At Home in the Sky

THE AVIATION ART OF FRANK WOOTTON

Mary Henderson Valdivia Published for the National Air and Space Museum by the Smithsonian Institution Press

Library of Congress Cataloging-in-Publication Data:

Valdivia, Mary Henderson.
   At home in the sky.

   Catalog of an exhibition held at the National
Air and Space Museum, Sept. 15, 1983-Sept. 15, 1984.
   Supt. of Docs. no.: SI 9.2:SK9
   1. Wootton, Frank A. A.—Exhibitions. 2. Aeronautics
in art—Exhibitions. I. Wootton, Frank A. A.
II. National Air and Space Museum. III. Title.
ND497.W76A4 1984   759.2   84-600086
ISBN 0-87474-935-2 (pbk.)

This book was edited by Ruth W. Spiegel and designed by Alan Carter.

The paper in this book meets the guidelines for permanence and durability
of the Committee on Production Guidelines for Book
Longevity of the Council on Library Resources.

Front cover: *"Steady There! Them's Spitfires!"*, 1980.

Back cover: *Daylight Raid over Germany: B-17's Escorted by Mustangs*, 1976.

Contents

Acknowledgments

The author wishes to express her thanks to the following persons who assisted in the preparation of this book and in design of the exhibition: Walter J. Boyne, Director; Barbara Brennan, exhibit designer; Richard Crawford, former Chief, Exhibits Division; Patricia Graboske, editor; Dale Hrabak, photographer; Robert van der Linden, researcher; and Helen McMahon, publications coordinator. The assistance of the Royal Air Force is especially appreciated for providing transport for many of the paintings in the exhibition.

Special thanks to the following authors for permission to use quotations from their articles:

John Blake, *The Aviation Art of Frank Wootton*, edited by David Larkin (Peacock Press/Bantam Books, 1976).

Paul Brickhill, *Reach for the Sky: The Story of Douglas Bader* (W. W. Norton and Company, 1954).

Adolf Galland, *The First and the Last*, translated by Mervyn Savill (Methuen and Co., 1955).

Victor Head, "Frank Wootton, Flying's Own Ace Artist," *Hand-in-Hand: The International Journal of Commercial Union Assurance* 2:8 (August 1978).

Laurence Irving, O.B.E., letters to author of July 2, 1983, and January 9, 1984.

James Laver, "The Mirror of the Passing Show," *The Studio* 144 (July/December 1952).

James Sweeney, "Art Exhibit Soars at the Smithsonian," *Montgomery Journal*, October 20, 1983.

Foreword

I first saw Frank Wootton's paintings in 1977 while visiting the Royal Air Force Museum in London. At that time, I was particularly impressed by *Hawker Harts over the Himalayas* (plate 13), showing the Royal Air Force 11 Squadron of the North West Frontier Province, India, in 1935. The subject matter of this painting has an undeniable attraction for aircraft buffs; but more important, the quality of the painting itself interests all who view it. The complex and intriguing shapes, luminous light and color, and careful composition reveal the talent of the artist. In all of his paintings, Wootton effortlessly combines this visual beauty with factual accuracy and emotional appeal.

The National Air and Space Museum, at last, has had the opportunity to bring together 58 paintings by Frank Wootton for his first major retrospective exhibition. Not only is this the first time that all these works have been seen together, but this is Wootton's first major exhibition in the United States. As a group of historical documents, the paintings are unique, but primarily their impact is one of visual beauty. The range of emotions expressed in this collection of Wootton's canvases is compelling: elation, fear, excitement, nostalgia, and delight. His works communicate a sense of history, as well. It has given me great pleasure to see these works brought together for everyone to enjoy.

Walter J. Boyne
Director,
National Air and Space Museum

Introduction

Frank Wootton has been termed the foremost aviation artist of today. As president of the British Guild of Aviation Artists, he has great influence on other artists, and his book, *Drawing Aircraft*, is a classic in the field.

Wootton's hangar and runway scenes take the form of the classic "landscape with figures," and his style, a "romantic realism," is rooted in the tradition of English landscape painting. Influenced by eighteenth- and nineteenth- century artists such as Gainsborough, Constable, and Turner, Wootton is concerned with the intangible qualities of a scene—conditions of sky, light, and atmosphere—and the ever-changing drama of sunlight, wind, and clouds. Artist and writer Laurence Irving states that: "To paint sunlight in England with its variable and constantly changing climate requires exceptional courage and patience, yet Wootton revels in the problem. His landscapes, like the rest of his work, are forthright and brilliant."[1]

While based on observable facts, Wootton's paintings emphasize the sweeping forces of nature that create the mood and drama of the scenes he depicts. The sky becomes, in the words of Constable, "the key note, the standard scale, and the chief organ of sentiment." Constable went on to write that the "landscape painter who does not make his skies a very material part of his composition neglects to avail himself of one of the greatest aids";[2] and it is Wootton's use of this advice that makes his aircraft seem to float so gracefully in the wide expanse of the sky.

CHAPTER I

A Career in Art

FRANK WOOTTON is well known for his paintings of landscapes and horses, as well as for his aviation subjects. No matter what subject matter he treats, Wootton emphasizes the emotional qualities of a scene as well as the factual, combining expressive meaning with technical accuracy. He is an artist of remarkable versatility. As Victor Head has said, he paints "with vigor and panache subjects as diverse as a jet fighter taking off, the Calgary Stampede, or the ancient church a mile down the road."[3]

Much of his success comes from the fact that Wootton draws his imagery from what he sees and knows, then paints it with an emotive beauty that evokes a meaningful response. He states that "I am always seeking first-hand knowledge, for an artist can never rightly employ anything he does not understand. I paint mainly Sussex landscapes because I have always lived in Sussex (with, of course, occasional excursions elsewhere). When I wanted to paint the Royal Air Force, I joined it. When I painted horses I bought them, groomed them, rode them, and used them for models and bred my own foals, long before I ever painted horses that were not mine."[4]

Long-time friend Bill Warner has observed that Wootton possesses an "uncanny ability to capture a scene in his mind's eye and then reproduce it accurately on canvas a few days later. You'll notice his gaze focus on something in mid-sentence and briefly you feel that he's no longer with you. But he then continues the conversation without a hitch and you know that locked away in his head is a landscape or cloud detail that he'll reproduce in his studio next morning."[5]

Wootton lives near the village of Alfriston in Sussex, England, in the home he designed and built in 1955. Nearby is Windover Hill, the site of the chalk figure known as the Long Man of Wilmington, and the surrounding countryside of the Sussex Downs: the trees, meadows, animals, and gentle curves of the Cuckmere River that are featured in so many of his paintings. His pine-paneled studio, set apart from the main house among fir trees, is carpeted with oriental rugs and contains tables and chairs he has carved in oak. A view from the studio can be seen in the painting "*Steady There! Them's Spitfires*" (front cover).

Frank Wootton was born in 1914, in nearby Eastbourne, and demonstrated an early interest in drawing. Whenever he had the opportunity, he would sketch small scenes from nature such as clouds, flowers, and farm animals. At the age of 11, he was invited to attend the local Eastbourne College of Art, and at 14 was offered a scholarship there; against his parents' advice, he took it. As Wootton states, "My father was a very hard character and was with [the] Royal Navy all his life. He wanted me to become an architect or an engineering draughtsman if I had to take up drawing as a career. I was told that to be an artist was to work in a garret or on the pavement."

Nevertheless, Wootton was determined to pursue a career in the fine arts. At that time, Eastbourne College of Art was one of the best in the country. The training was academic, and included life-drawing, architecture, architectural perspective, the history of art, landscape painting, life-painting, design, and modeling sculpture. His chief inspiration was the study of the old masters, for whom he had a profound admiration. He studied their work at the National Gallery, the Tate, and the Victoria and Albert Museum. He assimilated much from these sources and made rapid progress with his art training.

Wootton won a Gold Medal and a traveling scholarship at the age of 17, and left the College in 1932 at the age of 18, launched now on his career as a free-lance painter and illustrator. The originality and competence of his style soon attracted commissions in advertising and publishing, and automobile and aircraft manufacturers were quick to recognize that his skills as an artist could enhance the quality of their pictorial advertisements.

It was taken for granted in his family circle that he would pursue an artistic career, yet the resources were not available for his tuition to the Royal College of Art. Wootton tells the following story: "I had to get some employment so [I] traveled to London with my folio.

Although it was the depression of the 30s, and it was difficult to find employment, I was lucky and started work in a commercial studio. I was like any other lad of my age; interested in cars and airplanes, and at that time there were many land and air speed records being broken. My interest in these events paid off for I was given work to do advertising these record-breaking flights and races for the petrol companies and other interested manufacturers.

"When the Ford Motor Company started manufacture in England with a large plant at Dagenhem, Ford sent over their advertising executives to find an advertising agency in the U.K. to carry out similar work to that in America. The studio in which I was working at the time was given a test advertisement and I was handed the work to do just as I was leaving at 6 p.m. I was told it was competitive and that every other studio in London was competing for the Ford account, so I stayed on and worked through the night, finishing up at 3 a.m. I walked seven miles home as the London buses and Underground were not running at that early hour. The next morning, arriving back at the studio, I learned that we had been awarded the account. This attracted other car manufacturers and I later carried out work for practically every car manufacturer in Great Britain, including Rolls Royce, also Volvo in Sweden and Renault in France."

But after three years, Wootton became restless doing so much advertising work and wished to work on his own. In addition, he longed for the Sussex countryside of his home. He had, in fact, bicycled the 60 miles home every weekend to his beloved Sussex. Wootton found that the landscapes he most enjoyed painting were also those where he would most enjoy living, and so returned to Eastbourne as a free-lance artist. He says of this period, "I painted cars to live, and lived to paint aircraft. As I was then fairly well known in the advertising field, I began to set my sights on the aircraft manufacturers. I had a great interest in flying; I made model aircraft, both scale and flying models, long before manufactured kits were sold."

During this time, he learned to fly at Wilmington and Shoreham. Both airfields had light aircraft, Avros and Tiger Moths, and the hours of flying time he logged helped him to establish a visual repertoire of flight images that would be of assistance later in his career. Wootton was painting these and other aircraft, such as the Hawker Demon (plate 1), for his own pleasure, but it was not long before some of his paintings were seen by representatives of the de Havilland Aircraft Company, and in 1935 he received what was to be the first of many commissions to execute pictures of aircraft. Other commissions soon followed in rapid succession, because, as Wootton says, "at that time no one really painted aircraft. If you opened an aviation magazine such as *Flight* or *Aeroplane*, the only advertisements were drawings by mechanical draughtsmen, which met requirements that are now taken care of by photography. Therefore it was fairly easy for anyone interested to take a more serious view of presenting the aircraft that were being constructed at the time." Wootton could also represent motor vehicles convincingly—he recollects that "few young students showed any interest in these subjects or had the capacity to express themselves in this direction"—and his ability won him numerous contracts.

Wootton was also commissioned to do the first Spitfire brochure, and received commissions from Vickers Armstrong, Bristol Aircraft, Handley Page, de Havilland, Airspeed, Fairey, and Rolls Royce. In his words, "I cannot think of a company I did not do anything for."

In 1939, with the approach of war, he volunteered for the Royal Air Force. This was a serious commitment for the artist. "There are certain major decisions one must make throughout life, and this was one of them. I knew that I would have to leave behind the beginnings of an interesting and lucrative career, but I realized I could not stay on the outside. If I was going in, I wanted to go my way." One of the things Wootton did was to find a home in Alciston, which is, in fact, only a little over a mile from where he lives now. "I took a small derelict 16th-century cottage in the country at Alciston, one of my favourite

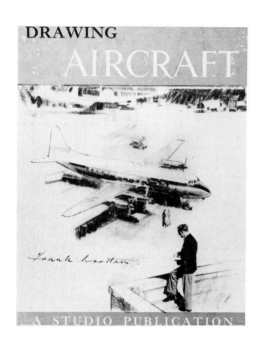

painting spots. The builder charged me twice as much as he had estimated on repairs to the cottage; fortunately I had written a small book for Studio Publications on *How to Draw 'Planes*, later retitled *Drawing Aircraft* (fig. 1). This little book sold out in two weeks and was reprinted, only to be sold out again in another few weeks. It was again reprinted, in fact seven times, and with the royalties I paid for the renovations to my cottage and entered the Royal Air Force without being in debt."

The Propeller Division of de Havilland Aircraft Company commissioned six paintings, showing the Spitfire, Hurricane, Blenheim, Wellington, the Sunderland Flying Boat, and the Defiant. These were war illustrations "based on combat reports" provided by the Ministry of Information. But Wootton did more than illustrate the combat reports—he expressed emotions and themes that were of deep meaning to the English people at that time. One of these paintings, *Defiants Enroute to Dunkirk* (plate 2), is for Wootton "a symbolic picture of the period when we had our backs to the wall. The heavy storm cloud expressed for me the state we were in at that time, when Churchill said: 'We shall fight on the beaches, we shall fight on the landing grounds . . . we shall never surrender,' and 'I have nothing to offer you but blood, toil, tears, and sweat.'[6] Then we sent some Defiants over—they were a new aircraft for us—and caught the Germans by surprise. That was the sort of scene you saw all over England; they were plowing up the fields, some fields that had never been plowed before, and we were sowing, for we knew there were going to be shortages, as shipping was being sunk at an alarming rate."

While waiting to be called up, Wootton was given the job of illustrating various "otherwise unrecorded" aspects of the war for the Ministry of Information and various magazines. Wootton was assigned to illustrate technical training manuals as well.

In 1940, at the invitation of Air Commodore Harald Peake, the director of Public Relations for the Royal Air Force, Wootton visited RAF stations to record the activities of the Royal

Air Force and the Royal Canadian Air Force. When he entered the RAF at last, he was unable to get an assignment abroad, because his technical drawings were so useful to the Training Command in instructing recruits.

Major Inspection of a Westland Lysander (fig. 2) of 400 Squadron at Odiham, Royal Canadian Air Force, was one of the first paintings Wootton executed as an official war artist. While he was working, the Engineering Officer came in and noticed that there was an oil slick on the floor, and that the artist had recorded it faithfully in his painting. The officer told the man seen working in the background to clean up the slick. When that was done, the officer returned to Wootton and requested him to remove it from his painting, and so he did. Wootton recalls that "they were very proud of the way they kept their aircraft and the hangars, too. They felt they were being inspected, and (rightly, as it turned out) recorded for posterity."

In 1944, Wootton was summoned to the Supreme Headquarters of the Allied Expeditionary Force, at Bentley Priory in Stanmore. He met the Commander-in-Chief of the Allied Tactical Air Forces, Sir Trafford Leigh-Mallory, and was invited to accept a special commission to go to France to record the work of the RAF during the battle for Europe. Laurence Irving feels that: "It was a period in which considerations of style and genre claimed an excessive and disproportional interest . . . among some of the artists appointed by the War Artists Advisory Committee. Wootton, faced with the realisation of his dreams, adopted an approach with humility and respect for the men and their machines involved in the greatest struggle for freedom in the history of mankind."[7]

Within three days of his appointment, Wootton was at an airstrip in Normandy—that of 35 Reconnaissance Wing. He shared the life of the pilots, and won their confidence and admiration as he illustrated vividly and accurately their aircraft in action, and the maintenance of them in the field as well. The painting *Mustang . . . Photographing a V.1 Site in the Pas de*

MAJOR INSPECTION ON A
"LYSANDER"
400 SQDN R.C.A.F.
ODIHAM

W.J. OTTON

19

Calais (fig. 3) dates from this time. Wootton attended briefings and interrogations and listened to the pilots' discussions of the tactical problems they had to resolve as they kept close watch on the German army. This gave him a profound understanding of the pilots' maneuvers as they closed on their targets and of their evasive action in the face of interception by the Luftwaffe. During this time, he became equally conversant with the tactical skills of the British army pilots, and their fighters and fighter-bombers.

Wootton traveled with a special pass, signed by the Commander-in-Chief, which gave him freedom of movement and transportation on anything available, including captured enemy vehicles. He was limited to 56 pounds of baggage, most of which was taken up by painting materials and rolls of canvas. Victor Head has said: "In the months that followed, Wootton learned what it was to paint in the most difficult conditions. He painted men and machines amid the uproar of battle. His wits and his vision were sharpened by necessity. He improvised in the most primitive conditions and his work, miraculously, retained its quality while acquiring a rare honesty and immediacy."[8]

John Blake tells an interesting story: "On one memorable occasion, [when Wootton was] painting under difficult conditions in Normandy and things were not going very well with the job in hand, an aircraftman who had been watching with great interest remarked on departing, "Ere, 'ave you read that book on 'ow to Draw 'Planes, by Frank Wootton?'"[9]

Wootton's war paintings provide a record for historians. Details such as the fact that 1944 was a very dry, hot summer, and that northern France was covered in white dust, are easily forgotten until one sees a Wootton painting of this period. Like the roads, the airstrips lay under a perpetual dusty cloud, and in it the Typhoons landed, rearmed, refueled, and took off. This is recorded in several paintings, such as *Typhoons, Normandy* (plate 3).

Mustang Maintenance, Normandy (fig. 4) shows the aircraft pulled off the dusty runway into the fields where the mechanics could work on them. The farmers worked around the aircraft

Figure 4   *Mustang Maintenance,*
Normandy, 1944.

and seemed determined to act as if all this were perfectly normal; so did the cows. Wootton felt that this was "one of the more peaceful scenes I thought should be recorded. It was painted at Fresny Folney, just north of Dieppe." While he was working on this painting, Wootton was given some cider to drink by one of the farmers in the background. This painting, incidentally, was damaged by shrapnel when the aircraft in which Wootton was flying was shot down over the English Channel on its way back to England, and this damage can still be seen on the right-hand side near the nose of the aircraft in flight.

But along with these peaceful moments, Wootton also witnessed scenes of death and devastation, such as that of *Typhoons at Falaise Pocket* (fig. 5). In August 1944, retreating German troops were surrounded and attacked by the Allies near the town of Falaise, France. The German 7th Army was virtually annihilated by attacks from the air, as long columns of armored and soft-skinned vehicles were destroyed. For Wootton, some aspects of the scene were unpaintable and he visually edited much of what he had seen, but nevertheless retained a sense of the horror. He says: "I went down to the battlefield with the pilots; the ground was littered with burnt-out vehicles and armour, some caught nose-to-tail in deeply cut roads. The gray-clad bodies of German soldiers were everywhere, some still in their vehicles sprawled over the seats, others on the running boards staring up into the sky, while in the neighbouring fields lay those who tried to seek safety off the roads. As the dust and smoke of battle would have prevented any photographer obtaining an overall picture, it had to be painted, although I omitted a great deal of the unpaintable."

In 1944 Wootton was invited to accompany Sir Trafford Leigh-Mallory to the Far East, where he had been appointed Commander-in-Chief. A seat was available on Leigh-Mallory's private aircraft (an Avro York), but Wootton had an uneasy feeling about the offer. He requested permission to return to Belgium first to collect the materials he had left there, and to follow the Commander-in-Chief at a later date. As it happened, the Avro York with

Figure 5   *Typhoons at Falaise Pocket*,
1944.

Sir Trafford and Lady Leigh-Mallory and their staff was lost in the Apennines in a snowstorm.

Wootton went on to Calcutta, India, and then traveled to Salbani. *Engine Change, Salbani, India* (plate 4) represents a typical scene from this period. The hot, dry, dusty conditions are reflected in the handling of the paint and the sharp contrasts of light and shade. The shortage of equipment and regular supplies is evident, as the engine is being serviced on the ground. The planes had to be serviced as much in the shade as possible, because the temperature of the metal skin could rise to dangerous levels in the sun.

Wootton painted Liberators bombing Rangoon, and recorded Spitfires and Mosquitoes attacking the Japanese from airstrips flooded by the monsoon in Mingaladon. Victor Head tells us that "he slept on a home-made stretcher of bamboo supported on two ammunition boxes. Colleagues laughed, but when the monsoon broke they awoke lying in inches of rainwater while Frank and his gear were high and dry."[10]

The RAF pilots considered it an honor to have their aircraft painted by Wootton, and often rivalries existed, as can be seen in a comparison of the painting *Spitfires of the Royal Air Force 607 Squadron at Mingaladon, Rangoon, Burma* (fig. 6) and a photo of the artist at work (fig. 7). It represents the 607 Squadron, painted in the monsoon conditions of Burma, very difficult flying weather. "This is a photo of me at work that shows a different aircraft from the one in the painting. There was a certain amount of squadron rivalry, and some of the chaps working on the aircraft would substitute another while I was at lunch, to get their squadron painted."

Number 8 Staging Post, Meiktila, Burma (fig. 8) was painted from the wooden control tower, and still reminds Wootton of the day-to-day life in the Far East at that time. It was, in his words, "an important little staging post in central Burma. We took this station from the Japanese; they regained it from us overnight; we repossessed it the next day. Damaged aircraft can be seen in the background. Under that little bit of thatch in one corner, you

Figure 6   *Spitfires of the Royal Air Force
607 Squadron at Mingaladon, Rangoon,
Burma*, 1945.

Figure 7   Frank Wootton at work on a flooded airfield at Mingaladon, Rangoon, Burma, 1945.

could get a cup of tea, and that was also where you reported. The Dakota was the most important form of transport there; it was very difficult to get an airplane flight in those days. You put your name down for a trip up to central Burma, and when you eventually obtained a flight you felt extremely lucky to have been included on board. Once, when I was traveling up to Meiktila, just as we were taking off from Rangoon, the aircraft stopped and the officer with the manifest came up and asked 'Is there any single person on board?' It was so hard to get a place on a flight that I wasn't readily going to volunteer, having waited so long for that seat, but he eventually got me off-loaded, saying 'We'll send you up to Meiktila on the mail plane.' It was actually a far more interesting journey, and when I finally did arrive at Meiktila, I reported that I was supposed to have been on that earlier flight. They looked at me and said 'You *are* lucky—it hasn't arrived,' and it never did."

During his six months in Burma, Frank had several narrow escapes. While painting a pair of Thunderbolts taking off, he watched with horrified fascination as a 500-pound bomb became dislodged and headed straight for him, only to bounce over his head and land without exploding.

Quick portrait sketches were always in demand. Laurence Irving recalls that "he would sit in a Forces canteen with a queue of prospective sitters who would exchange their chocolate ration for these sketches." He also remembers that "this curious trait of swapping that originated in the Service sometimes reoccurred on later occasions. After the war, Wootton was asked to paint a Rolls Royce by a famous firm that built custom-made coachwork. Wootton agreed to do a painting of their car if they would repaint his Bentley, which had lost some of its pristine appearance. On another occasion he agreed to paint a square-rigged Brig, *The Royalist*, a training ship owned by the Sea Cadets Association, in return for a day at sea with a turn at the wheel. Many years later, when Wootton was asked by an Inspector of Taxes if he ever did work on the basis of barter, he confessed that he had given a

No 8 STAGING POST
MEIKTILA · BURMA
MAY 1945

WOOTTON

28

Figure 8   *Number 8 Staging Post, Meiktila,*
Burma, 1945.

neighbouring farmer a watercolor. When asked what he received in exchange, Wootton replied that he had accepted a cartload of cow manure for his roses."[11]

After the war, Wootton came home to find a variety of projects waiting for him, including finishing work painted in the field, and arranging for the framing and organization of the paintings for distribution to various Royal Air Force Headquarters and to the Imperial War Museum in London. He had not always been able to find proper painting materials, and had frequently used aircraft fuel as a medium to mix his paints. It had the advantage of drying quickly, which was useful in uncertain conditions. For example, while he was working on the painting *Retraction Test, Royal Air Force 355 Squadron Liberator, Salbani, India* (fig. 9), a sudden sandstorm sprang up. All of Wootton's kit and the painting itself were blown away in a cloud of sand while the artist sought shelter. Wootton later found the painting against a barricade, covered with sand, but the image was undamaged because the fuel mixed with the paint had dried it so quickly. Despite the usefulness of aircraft fuel as a medium, however, it did leave paintings with a dull, lifeless surface. After the war, Wootton was able to rectify this and revive them through judicious varnishing.

He was also asked to work on such diverse projects as consulting on the visual appeal of the body work of the Jaguar motorcar and designing the interior of passenger planes. Moran, the tugboat king of New York, invited Wootton over to put his fleet on canvas, and an international petroleum company commissioned 24 paintings of the Persian desert.

Wootton's influence abroad can be estimated from the invitation offered by Sir Hudson Fysh, who pioneered Qantas, the international airline of Australia. He wanted Wootton to fly out to Australia and paint his fleet of aircraft. Simultaneously, Wootton was being asked by the Society of British Aircraft Constructors to paint the latest British aircraft being manufactured after the war. Many of these were being converted from military to civil use by disposing of the gun turrets and bomb bays, and installing comfortable upholstery and

Figure 9   *Retraction Test, Royal Air Force 355 Squadron Liberator, Salbani, India, 1945.*

rows of windows. He was approached at the same time by British Overseas Airways (BOAC) to paint their fleet of aircraft. He carried out the work for the Society of British Aircraft Constructors and the British Overseas Airways. "I regret that I was unable to do anything for Qantas; it was a case of one pair of hands."

Wootton traveled all over the world on the BOAC routes to paint the aircraft at different destinations; one such painting is *Constellation Refueling at Kloten Airport, Zurich* (plate 5). Later, he painted only the destinations without any aircraft. Wootton greatly enjoyed this "pure landscape painting" as a much-needed break, and to do this he visited Africa, South America, Japan, Hong Kong, Singapore, the West Indies, Canada, and the United States. About this time, Wootton felt that he needed to seek new subjects to paint, and to move away from his primary focus on aviation.

One commission involving landscapes rather than aircraft was offered by the Cyprus government in 1950, for six landscapes of the island. A small exhibition was staged at Nicosia, and the governor of the island, Sir Andrew Wright, opened the exhibition. During this same period, Sir Alfred Munnings, who had noticed Wootton's paintings at the Royal Academy, came down to Sussex to meet Wootton in his studio. Wootton says, "It was about this time that Sir Alfred Munnings, president of the Royal Academy, came down to my cottage in Sussex and asked me to paint more horses. He stayed quite a while, I gave him some tea, we chatted about painting and painters. He wanted to award me with the David Murray scholarship (a traveling scholarship awarded by the Royal Academy), but I was traveling so much at the time that I felt I could not honestly accept it. I suppose we had been talking the best part of an hour when I asked Sir Alfred if his chauffeur would like some tea. He said he thought the chap could look after himself, but no doubt Lady Munnings might like some—he had left her sitting in the car in the farmyard all this time!"

Nevertheless, Wootton took Sir Alfred's advice regarding horses seriously. Wootton had ridden all his life and it seemed natural to turn to horses for inspiration. "I began to refuse further invitations to paint aviation subjects and bought some horses. . . . Taking Munnings advice, I bought my first horse as a model, Smokey, and then I bought a bay. I bought them to paint, and I rode them, of course. I was very reluctant to finally part with them. I've gotten too busy in the last few years, and it takes time to groom and exercise horses. I don't paint quite so many now." Wootton's first exhibition of his horse paintings was at the famous Ackermanns Gallery in Bond Street, London. All 40 of the paintings were immediately sold out, to his surprise.

For Wootton, this time out for painting landscapes and animals was vital. "It's a great relief, when one gets a little tired of machines, to paint something alive; horses and landscapes give you far more freedom than an engineering marvel. People know it so well that you've got to watch your step, whereas a horse can vary a little bit." He has, in fact, depicted animals from foxes and farm livestock to African bull elephants. "The prospect of painting horses appealed to me; clearly a living horse was more of a challenge. Aircraft are comparatively easy to portray, as they are static, symmetrical, and any competent draughtsman can create a tolerable painting of a flying machine. However, to take the painting of aircraft beyond the conventional illustration, one must study the principles of light, movement, and composition, and also have a close affinity with nature's myriad forms and light when painting skies. Of the aircraft itself, the ability to establish a correct relationship between broad effects and minutiae is of the utmost importance. Constable once said 'let the form of an object be what it may—light, shade, and perspective will make it beautiful.' Also, one cannot evade the third dimension, for without this important and stimulating factor a painting becomes merely superficial, as a great many imitations reveal."

But Wootton could not give up the lure of painting aircraft, and soon began to combine them with horses in landscape settings. *"Steady There! Them's Spitfires"* (front cover) is a scene from the bottom of his garden. Frank describes what is happening: "As it often happened during the war, particularly during the Battle of Britain, some German aircraft would escape from battle and would dive down to ground level and fly very, very low, through the trees and over the villages. The Germans used to count the ammunition of fighter aircraft on their return to see just what had been expended and to check the pilot's story of how much shooting he'd done. So to expend any remaining ammunition, they'd shoot at anything that happened to be on the ground, such as horses plowing or farmers or transport or anything they saw. Therefore, some of these farm horses got very nervous when they heard an aircraft pass. Here, the plowman has come round the front to steady the horses and he's saying to them 'steady there, them's Spitfires. No need to worry.'" This painting gives an insight into the war, and its effect on the people, that is not presented in the photographic documentation of the time.

Another recent work combining aircraft and horses is *Royal Air Force Fodder Drop to Snowbound Exmoor Ponies* (fig. 10) showing the tough Anchor herd of Exmoor ponies, which are kept out on the moor all year round. During the two big snowstorms since 1962, the ponies could not reach any food under the snow. The Royal Air Force sent helicopters to drop hay down to them, and Wootton illustrated this event as "just another one of the many tasks undertaken by the RAF." Wootton adds, "I dare say that it's another excuse for me to paint ponies."

The work of the Royal Air Force is of continuing interest to Wootton. He recently visited Sek Kong, Hong Kong, where he watched—and painted—the Royal Air Force training Gurkha soldiers and dogs used to intercept the infiltration of illegal immigrants into Hong Kong (fig. 11).

Wootton feels that the time he spends painting horses, landscapes, and other subjects ultimately has an important, positive effect on his aviation work. "While exploring other

Figure 10   *Royal Air Force Fodder Drop to Snowbound Exmoor Ponies*, 1982.

Figure 11 *Royal Air Force Training Gurkha Soldiers with Dogs, Sek Kong*, 1982.

fields—and it must be remembered that my academic training had widened my interests in art—I did not entirely desert my interest in aviation painting, although I was spending less time on aircraft subjects and was pursuing more objective ends. By taking infinite pains with new compositions and experimenting with fresh approaches, I found that this break in other directions led to a stimulus towards new goals. This direct approach to nature continues in the study of natural appearances, evolving new methods of recording them in paint."

Wootton recently has painted several reminiscent works, such as *Daylight Raid over Germany: B-17's Escorted by Mustangs* (back cover) and *The Battle of Britain, September 15, 1940* (plate 6). He continues in his role as president of the British Guild of Aviation Artists, and John Blake reports that "his annual reports as chief judge of the major competitions and exhibitions are valued documents. It is in this particular sphere of activity, perhaps, that one of his most outstanding characteristics is revealed, for no artist can have been so generous of his time and talent in advising the many Guild members, professional as well as amateur, who come to him for aid."[12]

CHAPTER II

The Artist and His Style

I T IS WOOTTON'S ATTITUDE toward the landscape and sky that gives life and meaning to his work. He sketches out of doors, under the immediate inspiration of nature, and thus retains direct spontaneity in his artistic statements. With his mastery of atmospheric effects, the sky becomes a mirror, reflecting the sweeping forces of nature with which man struggles for control, or in its infinite variety, a benevolent environment. As John Blake has said, "In this wide setting, his aircraft float, at home and natural."[13] Laurence Irving sums up the power of Wootton's work:

> Through the radiant impact of light on the texture of metallic surfaces, Wootton creates the illusion of weightlessness in the airborne craft he depicts. The solidity of their structure and the source of their propulsion are dissolved by fleeting accents of light and shade. Yet he can convey the impression of an overburdened bomber straining to lift its load on takeoff, and his affinity with pilots and his familiarity with the performance of their aircraft enables him to interpret precisely and authentically military operations described to him by the combatants. Wootton's awareness of the significance of every aspect of aviation is a vital part of his mastery of this genre.
>
> Suffused with light, these paintings offer an amazing scope of atmospheric features. The summits of cumulus peaks seem substantial in their sculptural grandeur—forbidding canyons of air cleave the density of thunderclouds in contrast with the dappled beauty of cirrus ceilings. Whispy mare's tails herald a storm, and diaphanous curtains of rain screen the earth while they are softly illumined by the clear sky above."[14]

As James Sweeney has said, "Wootton portrays not just aircraft, but also the awesome beauty and special lighting of the atmosphere. He is as much a painter of light as he is of aircraft. At times he approaches the quality of the Luminist painters such as Frederick Church and Albert Bierstadt in his handling of light and clouds."[15]

Wootton himself places an emphasis on the importance of weather in his compositions, as it is of primary concern to the pilot whenever he flies. Wootton states that "most of my paintings depend largely on the sky for a very material part of the composition. All landscape painting is weather and the sky gives scale to a painting, and luminosity. The interplay of sunlight and shadow is one of the most valuable assets to composition."

Wootton also feels deeply about the importance of the landscape in any painting he completes. He says, "You can't alter your style when painting landscape—it's something that is like your own handwriting."

Composition is of enormous influence in the creation of his expressive paintings. "In the construction of a picture, composition is the first thing I look for, and then a sense of scale. The whole atmospheric balance of the picture must be consistent throughout the work; the governing quality is the spontaneous reaction to the transient loveliness of the visual scene, those fleeing effects of light which come and go so swiftly." Wootton works directly from nature or from his memory of things he has witnessed, rarely from photographs.

He describes how he goes about determining a composition. "In bright sunlight or on a grey day, a space of three to four miles can appear very flat, so I look for something to give me composition. I watch the clouds coming over the downs; the shadows fall and race across; sometimes a hill in the background or foreground will be in shadow and sometimes in sunlight. One must select what is best for the painting. The sky, of course, should always be an effectual part of the composition. Differences in lighting can be employed to give visual aids, both in colour and in perceiving the different shapes. I frequently repaint one view over and over again, as it changes all the time."

This use of a few simple elements to create an interesting and meaningful composition can be seen in a work such as *Looking for Trouble* (plate 7). The viewer is standing on the ground, looking up at the aircraft flying over. The arrangement of the clouds carefully balances the lines of the aircraft. The expressive clouds carry the action, and the immensity of sky and the sweep of the aircraft are expressed effortlessly. Wootton recalls: "That was just a typical scene; the RAF adopted that flight formation in those days. Later it was altered to a finger four formation. At that time our Spitfires were painted underneath half black and half white. Later on the eggshell blue was adopted."

Wootton's style is influenced by the classical tradition of English landscape painting, especially by the work of John Constable (1776–1837). Constable understood that the appearance of landscape is always changing with the movement of the sun and clouds. He once wrote that "painting is a science, and should be pursued as an enquiry into the laws of nature. Why then should not landscape painting be considered as a branch of natural philosophy, of which pictures are but the experiments?"[16]

A hallmark of Constable's style was the luminous subtlety, atmospheric effects, delicately shaded green hues of the English countryside in summer, and the smoky blues of distant hills (fig. 12). In addition, Constable sought perfection at what he called "its primitive source, nature," looking for subject matter under every hedge and in every lane, and thus modified ideas about what constitutes a beautiful landscape, in nature as well as in art. These ideas are reflected quite clearly in Wootton's attitude about art, as well as in his paintings.

Wootton's paintings are based on observable facts, and are reminiscent of Constable, "embodying a pure apprehension of natural effect." In Wootton's paintings one can almost sense the frost on a winter's day or the blossom in spring. Although he works quickly, he plans well ahead. He says of one of his paintings: "That's a view quite near here and I suppose it took me under three hours to complete. But those special conditions of late afternoon autumn light are found only at a certain hour towards the end of October. I was driving by two or three years ago and, as I didn't have time to stop, I made some notes in

Figure 12 *A View of Salisbury Cathedral* by John Constable, c. 1825 (oil on canvas). Andrew W. Mellon Collection. Reproduction courtesy of the National Gallery of Art, Washington, D.C.

a diary so that, perhaps, the following year I could return and, with luck, get the same conditions and paint the picture."

One painting of Wootton's that reflects Constable's pastoral scenes is the *Vickers F.B.5 "Gunbus"* (plate 8). Small details incorporated into the work lend it authenticity, such as the rain-filled rut in the foreground, and the routine activities in the background. These details also indicate the artist's concern for naturalism, and lend a feeling of immediacy and intimacy. This aircraft "portrait" was painted from a replica owned by the Royal Air Force Museum, which commissioned the painting. It looks back on World War I from the vantage point of the 1970s, incorporating a nostalgic feeling for the past. In the golden glow of the late afternoon sunlight, the aircraft wheel and turn on the breeze, and the war appears far away. It illustrates the different pace or tempo in the 1914–18 period, as opposed to the urgency exemplified in *Typhoons, Normandy* (plate 3).

Because of its idyllic atmosphere, the *Vickers F.B.5 "Gunbus"* can also be likened to the views of "Arcadian places" so dear to the hearts of the Romantic painters of the eighteenth century. They were, in turn, derived from the myth of the Golden Age, which had haunted the European imagination since antiquity.

The Romantic artists were united less by a specific style than by an attitude of mind prevalent at that time, which sprang from a craving for intense emotional experience. The declared aim of the Romantics was to "return to Nature—nature the unbounded, wild and ever-changing, nature the sublime and picturesque."[17] In the name of nature, the Romantic artists and poets worshiped liberty, power, love, and violence, as well as the milder extremes of the mythical Golden Age; actually, emotion as an end in itself. At its extreme, this attitude could be expressed only through direct action, not through works of art, as the creation of a work of art demands some detachment and self-awareness. What Wordsworth, the great

Romantic poet, said of poetry—that it is "emotion recollected in tranquillity"—applies also to the visual arts.

Wootton's relationship to the Romantic ideal lies in his unquestionable involvement with every subject that he chooses to depict, and his flair for seeking out the most dramatic moment in a narrative. He has an emotional investment in his settings and in his subjects. Wootton is in love with the environment he depicts, stating: "I look upon landscape painting as purely recreational. Living in a beautiful part of Sussex on the South Downs, I am surrounded by the most paintable subject matter, and when I ride out on my horse I note the time of day and the time of year when certain parts of the landscape are revealed to best effect. I make notes, and return with my paints at the first opportunity." For Wootton, the interest in a subject must come first and the desire to paint it later and, as he says, "I know what I want to do and toil incessantly to achieve my purpose."

A painting that expresses the Romantic concern for the sublimity of nature—in all of its exhilaration and terror—is *Defiants Enroute to Dunkirk* (plate 2). There is a mingling of despair and hope, heroism and a stubborn determination to survive, mirrored in the vastness of the sky, the lowering clouds pierced by shafts of sunlight. The aircraft seem tiny and fragile in this expanse, but express the same resolution to go on as the farmer does plowing his fields below, and the same faith in the endurance of England. This dramatic painting evokes an emotional response, highlighted by the dark clouds with the rays of light. The heroism of man is emphasized through the farmer, stoically plowing up the fields as the routine of daily life goes on. Here is a trait that can be discovered throughout Wootton's work—a concern for man caught up in the sweeping forces of nature. This is used to create the mood and drama of the scenes he depicts.

Wootton is also concerned with expressing a more reflective meaning, and using the ever-changing forces of nature to do so. The *Boeing B-17 Flying Fortress* (plate 9) is set in the vastness of the darkening sky, and dramatic contrasts in color give it an emotive feeling. Painted in 1965, it is a nostalgic look backwards at the 8th United States Air Force returning from a daylight bombing raid on Germany in 1943. The artist tells us that "this aircraft completed 25 operational missions from England and although badly damaged on numerous occasions by flak and fighter cannon fire, returned to the U.S.A."

This painting, however, is more than just a look back on a wartime scene. Its mystery is reminiscent of the words that Philipp Otto Runge, author of the most radical of Romantic theories of painting, wrote in 1802: "The sky above me teems with innumerable stars, the wind blows throughout the vastness of space, the wave breaks in the immense night . . . ."[18] Wootton tells us about the meaning of this work: "The Boeing B-17, on its way home, is badly shot up—this was a common sight after a daylight raid. Some of the aircraft would limp back and it was evident that they had been through an awful lot of punishment. Many of the aircraft were so badly damaged that you wondered how they could still be flown. The crew were so glad to get down, and on occasions I've seen Americans jump out of their aircraft and kiss the ground." There is about this artistic conception a sense of calm after turmoil, the peace felt after a victory scored in the struggle to survive. This impression is reinforced by the late afternoon glow, where the clouds seem to be made of spun gold and the sky takes on a greenish tint. Wootton carefully chose the timing for this scene: "The sun has left the ground, and the lights are just showing up on the airfield below, while the sun is still catching the top of the cloud. At that time of the day the cumulus cloud is decaying and falling, it's getting a little broken up down at the base and is losing its sharpness. It won't last much longer, perhaps in half an hour it will be gone altogether."

Wordsworth's poetry also comes to mind when viewing this painting:

. . . And I have felt
A presence that disturbs me with the joy
Of elevated thoughts; a sense sublime
Of something far more deeply interfused,
Whose dwelling is the light of setting suns,
And the round ocean and the living air,
And the blue sky, and in the mind of man:
A motion and a spirit, that impels
All thinking things, all objects of all thought,
And rolls through all things.[19]

James Sweeney states that "Wootton is most in his element when showing the action of aviation during war. While he does not glorify war . . . he does glorify the men and machines who go to war."[20]

CHAPTER III   *The Narrative Paintings*

WHILE WOOTTON PAINTS land and sky in the classic tradition, he is unmistakably of this century. Although his style is rooted in the past tradition of English landscape painting, his subjects are of his own time, and many represent narrative scenes he has witnessed or has had described to him first hand.

Like the Japanese "mirror of the passing show," Wootton tells us of the nature of our time, and invites the viewer to reflect on present-day themes. Wootton agrees that the key to the realism of his paintings is his extensive experience as a pilot: "To show an aircraft in action, you've got to know the limitations of that aircraft—what it can do in a turn and so on. The action must be shown from the best point of view at the critical moment, because obviously there are so many maneuvers that lead up to it. After that it's just a question of composition; you look at the thing in your imagination, you have the pilot's story, and it is just a matter of organizing it."

An example of how he translates words into dynamic scenes is the painting *Achtung Spitfire* (plate 10), created in 1978 to help raise funds for the Battle of Britain Museum (prints were made of this painting and sold). The action was described to Wootton by the two main combatants, and he then translated it into a visual image. He has chosen the moment when a formation of British bombers, accompanied by an escort of Spitfires, crossed the French coast at about 14,000 feet, prior to a bombing run on one of the airfields in 1940. Diving at high speed from a considerably higher altitude is Generalleutnant Adolf Galland (at that time a 28-year-old Oberstleutnant), leading aircraft from Jagdgeschwader 26 "Schlageter" down to attack the bombers. The close escort Spitfires are seen turning up to face the attack, while Wing Commander Stanford-Tuck of the Biggin Hill Wing, diving from a higher altitude, is just opening fire with his cannon on the leading Messerschmitt. Wootton has captured this split second in a fast-moving, constantly changing action, and illustrates vividly the tremendous speed, distance, and altitude of the fighter versus bomber action in a vast area of the sky. The commemorative signatures of the two pilots give historical authenticity.

It is a classical but dynamic composition. Strong diagonal lines pull the viewer into the painting, while a feeling of the tension of the moment is generated by the strong sweep of the clouds.

Wootton frequently works from stories he has heard from others, and states: "Of course, in a single seater and in fighter action, I couldn't have been with them. As soon as the pilots came back, they were debriefed by the intelligence officer. He wanted to know exactly what happened, who was shot down, and how many sorties there were. Listening to this first-hand account, one formed a clear mental picture. If there was anything else I wanted to know, the pilot would give me the rest of the details."

One example of this is the painting *Battle of the Dinghy* (plate 11). The inspiration for this painting came from a story about the capture of a German pilot, told to Frank Wootton by Squadron Leader Michael Robinson: "Two British air-sea rescue launches were attempting to rescue an important German aviator who had been shot down in the Channel and had taken to his dinghy. The rescue launches were attacked by Messerschmitt 109s, and one launch was set on fire. Four Messerschmitts were destroyed, plus two probables, for two Spitfires damaged."

The quality of light on the water, and the luminous reflections, give this painting its special appeal. To paint the scene, Wootton hung over a clifftop 600 feet above the water, and in his words, "I just painted the sea down below. Afterwards, I added the aircraft." To get the luminosity, impasto, and light on the water, he took a paraffin candle, melted it down, and mixed some of that into his paint; the wax gives it the brilliance of the light on the water. Wootton has remarked that "it is interesting to see the durability of this medium after a period of 43 years, as good as the day it was painted."

Another example of a historical rendering is the painting of the *Royal Air Force 617 Squadron Raid on the Möhne Dam, May 16, 1943* (plate 12). Painted 34 years after the event, it is an accurate depiction of the daring and difficult attack on the strategic Möhne Dam. Wootton researched the subject extensively, and selected the moment when Wing Commander Guy Gibson and his crew dropped the bomb designed by Dr. Barnes Wallis. The Avro Lancaster had been specially modified for this mission. It was equipped with a mechanism in the bomb bay which would spin the bomb as it was dropped, so that it would skip over the surface of the water and hit the wall of the dam. The bomb had to sink along the right point of the dam wall so that when it exploded, there would be enough water pressure behind the explosion to breach the dam completely. The placement of the bomb was vital to its success, and it was necessary for the aircraft to fly at an extremely low altitude of 60 feet, at a carefully calibrated speed of 232 miles per hour. The intersecting beams of light seen under the Lancaster enabled the craft to maintain its proper altitude. This attack on the Möhne Dam devastated the Ruhr Valley and cost the Germans several months of production.

Knowing the aircraft thoroughly also is important to the success of Wootton's paintings. An aircraft, like a human body, has a certain anatomy to it—it is in essence a framework covered with a skin. This anatomy is not readily apparent from the exterior, especially in modern aircraft, because the covering is smooth and metallic. To depict an aircraft in its sculptural roundness, a knowledge of engineering is necessary; this Wootton has from his studies. This is why his aircraft come across so naturally and three-dimensionally in his paintings.

Critic James Laver wrote in 1952 that "Frank Wootton is concerned with the streamlined elements of the modern scene. He concentrates upon the mechanical monsters themselves which, as they have grown more efficient, grow, reassuringly, more beautiful. The airplane has outgrown its awkward pterodactyl stage and evolved, rather surprisingly, into a gleaming

Figure 13   *Friday the 13th, Halifax,* 1978.

silver fish . . . to become the shape of speed—a thing beautiful in its own right."[21]

But Wootton does more than just render shining, factory-perfect aircraft. "I look for blemishes sometimes because then it shows that the aircraft has a few flying hours. In the painting of *Hawker Harts Over the Himalayas* [plate 13], you will notice that some of the polished metal has begun to discolour due to the hot exhaust." This painting also has an interesting story, as it was painted for the Royal Air Force Museum. They asked Wootton to paint any subject of his choice, from 1914 to 1945. He thought of the Hawker Harts, and remembered how he felt about them: "They looked beautiful on the airfield. I first saw them as a young art student and cycled 50 miles to Hawkinge to paint them. I was entranced to see a squadron of them on a field." For this painting, Wootton traveled to the North West Frontier where these aircraft, based in India, had operated in the 1935 era. From Risalpur he flew to Gilgit, Kashmir, in 1968 and painted the background; Nanga Parbat can be seen in the distance. He did not need to go so far for the aircraft: "the Hawker Hart was much nearer home, kept in flying condition at Dunsfold, Surrey." The pilots are wearing khaki polo topees instead of the usual flying helmets. They cut off the peaks in front so that they could slip their goggles on. The topees shaded the back of the neck, which easily could be badly sunburned in the tropics.

Wootton feels that "there are only certain types of aircraft I would want to paint in a nostalgic way, so that the onlooker could share the interest one has in expressing the shape, texture, and surface characteristics of metal and canvas to the point where one instinctively wants to touch it." One of these paintings, which has an interesting story, is *Friday the 13th, Halifax* (fig. 13). When the plane was first delivered on Friday the 13th, the crew took it as an omen of bad luck, and decorated the craft with bad luck symbols such as a skull and crossbones and an upside-down horseshoe. However, this plane had a highly successful career, completing all of its 128 operational sorties, and never losing a crew member. The clouds

Figure 14 *Bader Bail Out*, 1978.

are used to signal a message—dark clouds loom ominously, but the bright white ones in the back convey a positive outlook.

Wootton is interested in all types of aircraft, and states that "there is always something to admire in a successful aircraft, even an enemy one. It has its virtues just like a successful British fighter." For example, he painted a scene of *Operation "Bodenplatte"* (plate 14), the last ditch effort by the Germans to destroy the Allied air power on the ground. It is described by Generalleutnant Adolf Galland in his book *The First and the Last*. "In the early morning of January 1, 1945, every aircraft took off, some fighter units flying night fighters and bombers, and went into a large-scale well-prepared low-level attack on Allied airfields in the north of France, Belgium and Holland with the aim of paralysing the enemy's air force at one stroke. In good weather this large-scale action should have been made correspondingly earlier. The briefing order demanded the very greatest effort from all units. According to the records, about 400 Allied planes were destroyed, but the enemy were able to replace their material losses quicker than we were, and in this forced action we sacrificed our last reserves."[22]

Wootton's works also can be symbolic as well as historical. He uses the sweeping forces of nature, which create the mood and drama of the scenes he depicts, to emphasize the heroism of man in his struggle for survival. In a painting such as *Bader Bail Out* (fig. 14), the artist has chosen a psychologically intense moment in the story of Sir Douglas Bader. As a young pilot in the Royal Air Force, Bader had lost both legs in a flying accident in 1931. Nevertheless, he learned to fly again using his artificial legs, and was made a Wing Commander in World War II. In 1941, he was shot down over France, almost going down with the craft as one of his artificial legs became entrapped in the cockpit. Paul Brickhill, in his book *Reach for the Sky: The Story of Douglas Bader*, recounts the episode. "He struggled madly to get his head above the windscreen and suddenly felt he was being sucked out as the tearing

Figure 15   *Sea Harrier of the Royal Navy over the Falklands*, 1983.

wind caught him. Top half out. He was out! No, something had him by the leg, holding him. Then the nightmare took his exposed body and beat him and screamed and roared in his ears as the broken fighter dragging him by the leg plunged down and spun and battered him."[23] Bader managed to free himself in the nick of time, and was captured by the Germans. The Luftwaffe radioed England for a new leg, and this was delivered via a Blenheim during a bombing raid. He made numerous escape attempts, until the Germans had to place him in a maximum security prison in Germany for the remainder of the war. Wootton has chosen, out of this dramatic story, one psychological moment to sum up the whole—that moment when, his stricken plane uncontrollable and plunging to earth, he struggles to escape from the cockpit. In this battle against fate, he is using all of the resourcefulness he has learned in his fight to overcome his handicap. Bader becomes, in this painting, not just a man trapped by an accident, but a symbol of heroic endeavor against the overwhelming powers of nature.

Another example of Wootton's flair for capturing the drama of the moment is *Flight Lieutenant John Dundas Shooting Down Major Helmut Wick, Commander of JG-2* (plate 15). Wootton describes the setting: "John Dundas of the 609 Squadron (City of Yorkshire) had done an awful lot of flying, and he was showing signs of fatigue. While he did not admit it to himself, his medical doctor did, and stood him down to give him a break from flying duties. When Dundas heard that the squadron had been scrambled for a sortie over the Isle of Wight, he slipped over to the dispersal where his aircraft was and on the pretext that he was just giving it a test flight he took off and followed the squadron. Dundas joined the battle, and shot down the German ace Helmut Wick, who was credited with 56 victories. This was Dundas' 13th and last victory, for he was in turn shot down by the German leader's number two, who came out of the sun." Wootton has intensified the drama of the moment: as

Wick's craft plummets down the shape of his lieutenant's plane can be seen, coming out of a blaze of golden light.

While Wootton's early works are more symbolic, his later works depict more and more often scenes from everyday life. There is a sense of immediacy, as if the viewer is seeing a snapshot that freezes a particular motion forever. For example, Wootton recently depicted a Corsair coming off of the *USS John F. Kennedy* for a high speed run (plate 16). He did it from imagination, photographs, and the description of a friend. In his words: "I was in correspondence with Lt. Paul Pugliese of the U.S. Navy who had made many hundreds of flights from this carrier. He wrote to me and described to me exactly what went on and how they took off. I thought it a good exercise to paint this scene without having seen it, although I have been on board a British carrier at sea and watched aircraft take off and land. I sent him photographs as the painting progressed and he would put me right each time." The impression of speed and the illusion of motion is so compelling that it seems to be a still from a film. The composition is cut in such a way that it indicates that it is but a part of the workaday world. The bright, clear colors seem to provide the visual equivalent to the sharp sounds of takeoff, while the compositional technique, such as the way the plane cuts across the canvas at an angle, makes the viewer conscious of the world that must exist outside of the boundary of vision created by the frame.

Another recent work is of a *Sea Harrier of the Royal Navy over the Falklands* (fig. 15). In transit to the Falklands, the aircraft of the Royal Navy changed their usually dark camouflage to a pale grey color, to blend with the lighter color of the South Atlantic. The remains of the old markings can be seen faintly under the new coat of paint. While Wootton did not witness this action, he saw the aircraft at base, and wished to add this painting to his own pictorial history of the Royal Air Force.

Conclusion

Wootton's paintings owe their extraordinary power to his unique manner of seeing and representing, and their beauty cannot but evoke an emotional response. Much of this power comes from his own involvement in his work, for he has said that "like many other young men in those early days, I was fascinated with flying and the desire to fly. The desire to paint aircraft has just never left me." His visual subtlety, the frequent use of that strange intense polarity of closeness and distance, and the contrast of precise detail with atmospheric effects are feats of technical skill that Wootton uses to involve the viewer with the subject. His deep interest in the changing moods of landscape and sky, in the human drama of a narrative, and in the monumental in nature add meaning to his paintings. But above all, Wootton celebrates flying, in all of its exhilaration, delight, and joy. As Laurence Irving has said, "There has been no other painter of aviation in England with such a large output of work of such distinction to his credit."[24]

Plate 1   *Hawker Demon*, c. 1935 (watercolor).

57

Plate 2 *Defiants Enroute to Dunkirk*, 1940.

58

Plate 3   *Typhoons, Normandy*, 1944.

Plate 4 *Engine Change, Salbani, India*, 1945.

Plate 5   *Constellation Refueling at Kloten Airport, Zurich*, 1950.

Plate 6   *The Battle of Britain, September 15, 1940, 1983.*

62

Plate 7   *Looking for Trouble*, 1940.

Plate 8   *Vickers F.B.5 "Gunbus,"* 1973.

Plate 9   *Boeing B-17 Flying Fortress*, 1965.

Plate 10   *Achtung Spitfire*, 1978.

66

Plate 11   *Battle of the Dinghy*, 1940.

Plate 12   *Royal Air Force 617 Squadron Raid on the Möhne Dam, May 16, 1943*, 1977.

Plate 13 *Hawker Harts over the Himalayas*, 1968.

Plate 14   *Operation "Bodenplatte": January 1, 1945*, 1982.

Plate 15   *Flight Lieutenant John Dundas Shooting Down Major Helmut Wick, Commander of JG-2*, 1940.

71

Plate 16   *A-7 Corsair on the Launching Catapult, USS John F. Kennedy, 1983.*

Catalog of Artworks

The following artworks appeared in the exhibition *At Home in the Sky: The Aviation Art of Frank Wootton* at the National Air and Space Museum. All are oil, unless otherwise indicated. Those reproduced in this book are listed with a plate or figure number.

A-7 Corsair on the Launching Catapult, USS John F. Kennedy, 1983 (25¾″ x 30″). Collection of the artist. Plate 16.

Achtung Spitfire, 1978 (35½″ x 43½″). Collection of the artist. Plate 10.

Auster Landing at Headquarters Site, Normandy, 1944 (23½″ x 29½″). The Society of British Aerospace Companies.

Bader Bail Out, 1978 (31½″ x 39½″). Gift of the Smithson Society. Figure 14.

The Battle of Britain, September 15, 1940, 1983 (53¼″ x 7⅛″). Collection of the artist. Plate 6.

Battle of the Dinghy, 1940 (23¾″ x 29¼″). The Royal Air Force Museum, London. Plate 11.

Boeing B-17 Flying Fortress, 1965 (30¼″ x 35¼″). Collection of Henry O. Smith III. Plate 9.

Beaufighter Strike, 1943, 1983 (27⅜″ x 39¼″). Collection of the artist.

Breaking the Circle, 1982 (24⅜″ x 35⅜″). Collection of the artist.

Buccaneers over Gibraltar, 1982 (19¼″ x 29¼″). Collection of the artist.

Canadian Bush Pilot, 1982 (22½″ x 35¼″). Collection of the artist.

Constellation Refueling at Kloten Airport, Zurich, 1950 (20¾″ x 28¾″). Watercolor. Collection of the artist. Plate 5.

Daylight Raid over Germany: B-17's Escorted by Mustangs, 1976 (21⅜″ x 39½″). Collection of the artist. Back cover.

Defiants Enroute to Dunkirk, 1940 (21½″ x 29½″). The Royal Air Force Strike Command, Headquarters, High Wycombe. Plate 2.

Engine Change, Salbani, India, 1945 (14½″ x 25″). The Royal Air Force Museum, London. Plate 4.

English Landscape, Sussex, 1981 (20¼″ x 35¼″). Collection of the artist.

The First American Air Service Victories, 94th Aero Squadron, April 14, 1918, 1983 (24⅜″ x 35½″). Collection of Theodore Hamedy.

Flight Lieutenant John Dundas Shooting Down Major Helmut Wick, Commander of JG-2, 1940 (22¼″ x 26⅛″). The Royal Air Force Museum, London. Plate 15.

Friday the 13th, Halifax, 1978 (27½″ x 35½″). Collection of Victor Gauntlett. Figure 13.

Going Out with Hounds, 1975 (23⅛″ x 33½″). Collection of the artist.

Hawker Harts over the Himalayas, 1968 (27¾″ x 43⅝″). The Royal Air Force Museum, London. Plate 13.

Helicopter of the Royal Air Force 28 Squadron over Hong Kong, 1982 (19⅛″ x 29⅛″). Collection of the artist.

High Speed Run, USS John F. Kennedy, 1983 (21⅛″ x 39¼″). Collection of the artist.

The Horse Show, 1969 (19⅛″ x 39⅛″). Collection of the artist.

Horses by a Lake, 1971 (27½″ x 43⅛″). Collection of the artist.

Ilyushin Identification Sketch (1), 1950 (12¼″ x 15⅛″). Charcoal. Collection of the artist.

Ilyushin Identification Sketch (2), 1950 (12¼″ x 15⅛″). Charcoal. Collection of the artist.

Israeli Air Force F-15's in Action over the Bekaa Valley, 1982 (24⅜″ x 35¼″). Collection of the artist.

Javelins of the Royal Air Force 46 Squadron, Odiham, 1946 (25⅝″ x 29⅝″). The Royal Air Force, Headquarters Number 11 Group, Bentley Priory.

Knights of the Air: Sopwith Camel F.1s of the Royal Flying Corps 65 Squadron Engaging Fokker D VIIs of Jasta 11, 1979 (23⅜″ x 35½″). Collection of Victor Gauntlett.

The Last Combat, 1979 (23½″ x 35½″). Collection of Nick Maggos.

Lightnings of the Royal Air Force 56 Squadron, Wattisham, 1965 (41⅜″ x 53½″). The Royal Air Force, Headquarters Number 11 Group, Bentley Priory.

Looking for Trouble, 1940 (27¼″ x 39¼″). Collection of the artist. Plate 7.

Low Attack: Raid on the Engine Sheds at Trier, 1943 (23½″ x 29½″). The Royal Air Force, Officers' Mess, Marham.

Major Inspection of a Westland Lysander, Royal Canadian Air Force 400 Squadron, 1940 (18⅝″ x 26½″). The Royal Air Force Museum, London. Figure 2.

Mosquito Overshoot in the Jungle, 1945 (15⅜″ x 18″). The Royal Air Force Museum, London.

Mustang of the Royal Air Force 35 Photo Reconnaissance Wing Photographing a V.1 Site in the Pas de Calais, 1943 (21½″ x 29½″). Collection of the artist. Figure 3.

Mustang Maintenance, Normandy, 1944 (23⅜″ x 29½″). Collection of the artist. Figure 4.

Night Reconnaissance over Vietnam, 1978 (29½″ x 39½″). Gift of Phyllis S. Corbitt, in memory of Colonel Gilland W. Corbitt.

Number 8 Staging Post, Meiktila, Burma, 1945 (15¼″ x 18½″). The Royal Air Force Museum, London. Figure 8.

Operation "Bodenplatte": January 1, 1945, 1982 (24½″ x 35⅜″). Collection of Ramsay Milne. Plate 14.

Overshoot: Name? Number?, 1980 (19¼″ x 29¼″). Collection of Victor Gauntlett.

Retraction Test, Royal Air Force 355 Squadron Liberator, Salbani, India, 1945 (20½″ x 25″). The Royal Air Force Museum, London. Figure 9.

Royal Air Force Fodder Drop to Snowbound Exmoor Ponies, 1982 (24¼″ x 35⅜″). Collection of the artist. Figure 10.

Royal Air Force 617 Squadron Raid on the Möhne Dam, May 16, 1943, 1977 (35½″ x 47⅜″). The Australian War Memorial, Canberra. Plate 12.

Royal Air Force Training Gurkha Soldiers with Dogs, Sek Kong, 1982 (24¼″ x 35⅜″). Collection of the artist. Figure 11.

S.E.5a's of the Royal Flying Corps 56 Squadron, 1917, 1973 (21¼″ x 35⅝″). Collection of James B. Fleming.

Sea Harrier of the Royal Navy over the Falklands, 1983 (21¼″ x 29⅜″). Collection of the artist. Figure 15.

Spitfires of the Royal Air Force 607 Squadron at Min-galadon, Rangoon, Burma, 1945 (11⅛″ x 12″). Collection of the artist. Figure 6.

"Steady There! Them's Spitfires!", 1980 (23¼″ x 29¼″). Collection of the artist. Front cover.

Supermarine Spitfire Mk. V, 1982 (25″ x 35⅞″). Collection of Richard Lieberman.

Their First Flight: Air Training Corps Cadets, 1980 (27½″ x 29⅜″). The Royal Air Force Training Corps, Regional Headquarters, Central and East, Henlow.

Typhoons at Falaise Pocket, 1944 (41¼″ x 59½″). The Imperial War Museum, London. Figure 5.

Typhoons of the Royal Air Force 121 Wing Taking Off through Normandy Dust, 1944 (25⅜″ x 35¼″). Collection of the artist.

Typhoons, Normandy, 1944 (29½″ x 41¾″). Collection of the artist. Plate 3.

USAF F-16s, 1983 (27½″ x 39¼″). Collection of the artist.

Vickers F.B.5 "Gunbus," 1973 (27⅜″ x 43¼″). The Royal Air Force Museum, London. Plate 8.

V/Stol Harrier, 1974 (22″ x 30⅛″). Collection of the artist.

Notes

1. Laurence Irving, O.B.E., Letter to author, January 9, 1984.

2. John Constable, quoted in H.W. Janson, *History of Art* (New York: Prentice-Hall and Harry N. Abrams, 1962), p. 577.

3. Victor Head, "Frank Wootton, Flying's Own Ace Artist," *Hand-in-Hand* 2:8 (August 1978): 26.

4. From interviews conducted by the author and recorded on tape, and a letter to the author of October 12, 1983. Excerpts are quoted through this work.

5. Bill Warner, quoted in Victor Head, "Frank Wootton, Flying's Own Ace Artist," p. 26.

6. Winston Churchill, speeches at the House of Commons, June 4, 1940, and May 13, 1940, respectively.

7. Laurence Irving, Letter of January 9, 1984.

8. Victor Head, p. 28.

9. John Blake, *The Aviation Art of Frank Wootton*, edited by David Larkin (Peacock Press/Bantam Books, 1976), p. 9.

10. Victor Head, "Frank Wootton," p. 30.

11. Laurence Irving, Letter of January 9, 1984.

12. John Blake, *The Aviation Art of Frank Wootton*, p. 13.

13. John Blake, *The Aviation Art of Frank Wootton*, p. 5.

14. Laurence Irving, Letter to the author of July 2, 1983.

15. James Sweeney, "Art Exhibit Soars at the Smithsonian," *Montgomery Journal*, October 20, 1983, p. B3.

16. This and other Constable quotations in this section are from Hugh Honor, *Romanticism* (Harper and Row, 1979), pp. 63-65.

17. Janson, *History of Art*, p. 557.

18. Letter from Philipp Otto Runge to his brother Daniel, 1802, as quoted in Hugh Honor, *Romanticism*, p. 73.

19. William Wordsworth, "Lines composed a few miles above Tintern Abby," 1798.

20. James Sweeney, p. B3.

21. James Laver, "The Mirror of the Passing Show," *The Studio* 144 (July/December, 1952), p. 52.

22. Adolf Galland, *The First and the Last*, translated by Mervyn Savill (Methuen and Co., 1955), p. 319.

23. Paul Brickhill, *Reach for the Sky: The Story of Douglas Bader* (W. W. Norton and Company, 1958), p. 221.

24. Laurence Irving, Letter of January 9, 1984.